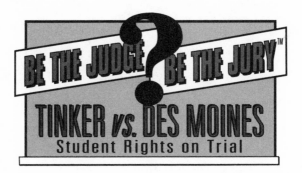

Also by Doreen Rappaport

LIVING DANGEROUSLY
American Women Who Risked Their Lives for Adventure

ESCAPE FROM SLAVERY
Five Journeys to Freedom

AMERICAN WOMEN
Their Lives in Their Words

THE BOSTON COFFEE PARTY

TROUBLE AT THE MINES

Be the Judge • Be the Jury
THE LIZZIE BORDEN TRIAL

Be the Judge • Be the Jury
THE SACCO-VANZETTI TRIAL

BE THE JUDGE? BE THE JURY™

TINKER vs. DES MOINES
Student Rights on Trial

DOREEN RAPPAPORT

ILLUSTRATED WITH
PHOTOGRAPHS, PRINTS
AND DIAGRAMS

HarperCollins*Publishers*

Grateful acknowledgment is made to the following for the use of photographs in this book.

The Bettmann Archive: 17. Collection of the Supreme Court of the United States: ix, 97, 112. *Des Moines Register*: 22, 23, 24, December 22, 1965; 27, January 4, 1966; 96, October 15, 1967. Chris Eckhardt: 28, 29, 38, 65, 132, 133, 134. Mary Grefe: 136. Dick Moberly: 82, 138. North High School Yearbook 1965: 18, 19, 40, 41, 43, 68. Doreen Rappaport: 14, 15. Katherine Tegen: 74, 86. Theodore Roosevelt High School Yearbook 1965: 18, 19, 26, 27, 60, 61, 62, 69, 72. Mary Beth Tinker: 37, 53, 88, 142. John Tinker: 140.

Tinker vs. Des Moines
Student Rights on Trial
Copyright © 1993 by Doreen Rappaport

1   2   3   4   5   6   7   8   9   10

First Edition

Library of Congress Cataloging-in-Publication Data
Rappaport, Doreen.
    Tinker vs. Des Moines ; student rights on trial / Doreen Rappaport.
        p.   cm. — (Be the judge/be the jury)
    Includes bibliographical references and index.
    Summary: Using edited transcripts of testimony, re-creates the trial of John Tinker and two other students who were suspended from school for protesting the Vietnam War, and invites the reader to act as judge and jury.
    ISBN 0-06-025117-4. — ISBN 0-06-025118-2 (lib. bdg.)
    1. Tinker, John Frederick—Trials, litigation, etc.—Juvenile literature. 2. Des Moines Independent Community School District—Trials, litigation, etc.—Juvenile literature. 3. Freedom of speech—United States—Juvenile literature. 4. Students—Legal status, laws, etc.—United States—Juvenile literature. 5. Vietnamese Conflict, 1961–1975—Protest movements—Iowa—Des Moines—Juvenile literature.   [1. Tinker, John Frederick—Trials, litigation, etc. 2. Trials. 3. Freedom of speech. 4. Vietnamese Conflict, 1961–1975—Protest movements.]   I. Title.   II. Series: Rappaport, Doreen. Be the judge/be the jury.
KF228.T56R37   1993   92-25019
342.73'0853—dc20   CIP
[347.302853]   AC

For those who protested the Vietnam War,
for those who fought in the Vietnam War,
for those who died in the Vietnam War

Contents

Everything in this book really happened. This book contains the actual testimony and briefs of *Tinker vs. Des Moines.*

Before the Trial

In 1965 American soldiers were fighting in South Vietnam in Southeast Asia. Many Americans supported this war. Some didn't. They protested by giving speeches and marching in demonstrations. Thousands of young men refused to go into the army.

In December 1965 twelve teenagers in Des Moines, Iowa, decided to wear black armbands to school to mourn the dead in Vietnam on both sides. School officials thought this might cause trouble, so they banned the wearing of armbands. The students wore them anyway. All were sent home from school. Five were officially suspended.

Three students sued the school officials. They believed that wearing the armband was a form of speech protected by the First Amendment to the U.S. Constitution. *Tinker versus The*

Des Moines Independent Community School District became one of the most famous students' rights cases in history.

For as long as it takes you to read this book, you will BE THE JUDGE. You will read the evidence and decide who is right—the students or the school officials. Read carefully. Think carefully about everything you read. Do not make your decision lightly, for you will decide the rights of all students for years to come.

Who Was Involved in the Tinker Case?

The three students who brought the lawsuit were fifteen-year-old John Tinker, thirteen-year-old Mary Beth Tinker (John's sister), and sixteen-year-old Christopher Eckhardt. The students were the *plaintiffs* in the lawsuit. Since they were minors (under eighteen years of age), the lawsuit was brought on their behalf by their fathers. John Tinker was the first plaintiff listed in the suit. The *defendants* were certain school officials involved in the suspensions, known collectively as The Des Moines Community Independent School District.

What Was the Vietnam War?

In 1965 a civil war raged in Vietnam, a divided country in Southeast Asia. The communist government in the North wanted the country reunified. Ngo Dinh Diem, the head of South Vietnam, did not want this. By December 1965 the Vietcong* was fighting in South Vietnam against Diem's army. The United States sided with Diem. President Lyndon B. Johnson and his advisors thought that if Vietnam "went communist," other countries nearby would also become communist. By the end of 1965, 200,000 American soldiers were fighting in the jungles in South Vietnam against the Vietcong.

*South Vietnamese Communists and non-Communist sympathizers with North Vietnam.

In 1965 How Did Americans Feel About the War?

This was the first time in history that a war had been shown on television on a daily basis. Every day millions of Americans turned on their televisions and saw thatched-roofed villages being bombed. They saw the dead bodies of men, women, and children. They saw innocent civilians running and screaming, their bodies aflame from bombs. The bombs contained napalm, a sticky substance mixed with gasoline. Napalm bombs were so powerful they could burn whole villages, destroy crops, and make it impossible to grow anything again for a long time.

Many Americans were horrified and shocked

by the destruction but feared communism so much that they believed the United States had to fight in this war. Some Americans did not approve of the war but believed that the president and his advisors would not have sent American soldiers to Vietnam unless it was absolutely necessary.

Some people were against the war. "Teach-ins" at colleges and universities presented the issues of the war to students. Many students became convinced that the United States did not belong in Vietnam. The students demonstrated against the war. They wore buttons with the peace symbol to show that they wanted peace. Some young men burned their

draft cards as a symbol of their refusal to fight. On November 2, 1965, a young man named Norman Morrison poured gasoline over his body, lit a match, and burned himself to death as a protest over the killings in Vietnam. That same month 25,000 protesters marched in Washington, D.C. Chris Eckhardt and his mother and John Tinker and his mother were on that march.

Burning draft cards to protest the Vietnam War

In 1965 How Did Americans Feel About Antiwar Protesters?

Americans who supported the war viewed these antiwar activities as horrifying, unpatriotic, unlawful, and wrong. They felt the protesters were betraying the American soldiers. Even some Americans who were against the war disapproved of the protests.

What Was It Like to Be a Student in Des Moines in 1965?

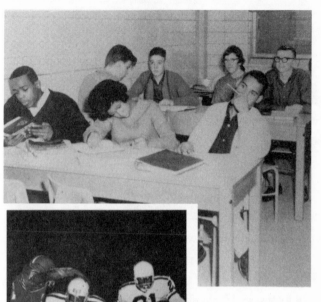

Aside from required classroom subjects, students participated in football, basketball, swimming, wrestling, cheerleading, dramatics, dances, chorus, band and orchestra.

As in most schools across the country, there was a dress code. Girls could not wear pants to school.

Their skirts had to be long enough so they would touch the floor when the girl kneeled down.

Boys had to cut their hair so it was not longer than the tops of their shirt collars. Jeans could not be worn by boys or by girls.

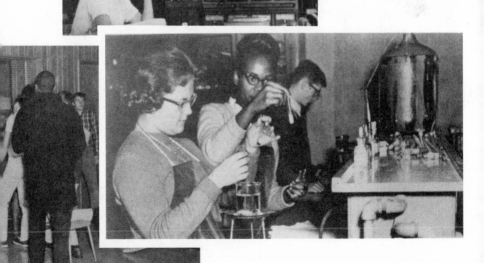

How Did the Case Get to Trial?

In early December 1965 some sixty Des Moines teenagers planned to wear black armbands to school to support a truce in Vietnam and mourn the dead on both sides. Ross Peterson, a student at Theodore Roosevelt High School, wrote an article about the armband demonstration for the school newspaper. His teacher told him that the article had to be approved by the principal because it was "controversial." When the principal learned of the possible armband demonstration, a meeting of all secondary-school principals was called.

The principals formulated a rule to ban armbands in school. All students wearing black armbands would be asked to remove them. If the student refused, his or her parents would be called and requested to ask their child to remove it. If that didn't work, the student would be sent home until the armband was removed or the policy was changed. Ross was told that his article would not be published.

Most of the students who had planned to wear the armbands became scared when they learned about the ban and decided not to participate. Some students telephoned the president of the school board and asked him to call an emergency meeting to hear their side of the case. He refused.

On December 16 and 17, twelve students wore armbands to school. Five were officially suspended. All were told they could not return until they removed the armbands or the school policy changed.

D. M. Schools Ban Wearing Of Viet Truce Armbands

Headline from the *Des Moines Register*

On December 21, 1965, two hundred people attended the regular monthly meeting of the school board.

The parents of Mary Beth and John Tinker and Chris Eckhardt had asked the Iowa Civil Liberties Union for help. The ICLU, an affiliate of the ACLU (American Civil Liberties Union), works to preserve the constitutional rights of Americans. The ICLU agreed that the students' right of free speech had been violated and hired Craig Sawyer to represent them.

Sawyer asked the school board to reinstate the students immediately, end the ban, and adopt a policy approving all forms of peaceable expression in school.

Chris Eckhardt with his parents

Mary Beth Tinker with her mother

A board member asked Sawyer, "Would you support students wearing Nazi armbands?"

"Yes," he answered, "and the Jewish Star of David and the cross of the Catholic Church and an armband saying, 'Down with the school board.'"

Some school board members were shocked by his answer. Tensions increased as other people for and against the armbands spoke.

Bruce Clark, one of the suspended students, said that in 1963 black armbands had been allowed in school to mourn the four black girls killed in a church bombing in Birmingham, Alabama. The school superintendent said the rule against armbands was not intended to ban the students' views on the war; the rule was adopted because the armbands might disrupt education. One citizen insisted the armbands meant a breakdown in proper conduct and school discipline. "If you don't have discipline, you don't have anything," he said.

A school board member moved to postpone a decision about the ban. Sawyer called out, "Take a stand! That's what you're here for!"

The board voted to extend the ban.

EXTEND BAN ON ARM BANDS

D. M. SCHOOL

Headline from the *Des Moines Register*

On December 23, 1965, the principals decided to continue the ban. They issued a memo explaining why:

1. A former student of North High was recently killed in Vietnam. Some of his friends are still in school. It is felt that if any kind of a demonstration exists, it might develop into something which will be difficult to control.

2. The schools hold appropriate assemblies on Veterans Day to honor the dead. Memorial Day is also recognized.

3. This rule follows standard procedure for what is considered inappropriate dress, haircuts, or other actions that attract attention.

4. Students at one high school were heard to say they would wear armbands of other colors if the black armbands were worn.

5. The schools are made up of a captive audience, and other students should not be forced to view the demonstrations of a few.

6. One principal reports a Nazi armband on a boy who came to school several weeks ago. When asked to remove it, he complied.

7. These students were sent home from school until they are willing to return without the armband. No student was suspended for a specified length of time.

The wearing of armbands was planned to last through the holidays, so the three students did not return to school until after Christmas vacation.

On Monday, January 3, 1966, several hundred people crammed the room for the next meeting of the school board. Antiwar sympathizers picketed the building. The meeting was noisy, and people heatedly spoke their views. This time the school board voted to uphold the ban.

Des Moines Board of Education

BAN ON ARM BANDS UPHELD

Headline from the *Des Moines Register*

Three students decided to sue the school board for violating their right of free speech. Under U.S. law, if a public official violates a citizen's constitutional right, that citizen can go to federal court and sue.

The trial was set for July 25, 1966.

Adults and teenagers expressed their feelings about the armband controversy in letters to the *Des Moines Register.*

Putting Arm Bands On Children

To the Editor:

. . . . Do the writers of the armband letters really believe the children involved arrived at their own decision to wear the bands? Do they believe the children had access to and had the intellectual maturity to undersand the significance of the complicated Viet Nam problem? Is it not more reasonable to suppose they were being used by their parents to publicize and foster the parents' opinions? . . .—**Rolf M. Heiberg, 3115 Mann ave., Des Moines 50310.**

'Liberty Dying'

To the Editor:

To the five School Board members who voted against permitting students to wear arm bands, may I observe that once again events indicated that our inalienable rights are indeed alienated; that liberty is dying an inch at a time.—**Elizabeth Ferrier, 821 Fortieth place, Des Moines.**

Says Consitution Is Violated

To the Editor:

It was stated that arm bands are a distraction to other students and instructors . . . John Tinker, did not try to make it known he was in mourning for those who have died in Viet Nam. He just attended his classes the same way he usually does, without disturbing a soul.

I believe a person may wear arm bands if he desires. The school board was in error in the sense that a person may do as he or she pleases, as set forth by the Constitution [particularly in] the First Amendment, which states Congress shall make no law respecting an establishment or religion, or prohibiting the free excercise thereof . . .—**Pat Parker, high school student 1628 Twelfth st., Des Moines.**

Called Shocking

To the Editor:

Again we have a shocking display of arrogant disdain for established authority, this time in Des Moines, in the persons of a minority group of students, parents, and questionable educators, who insist on a questionable right to wear black arm bands in mourning for those killed in Viet Nam. Whom do they mourn, our own or the Viet Cong? . . .

Those members of the school board who had the courage to stand up against this disregard of their decision against the wearing of the arm bands are to be commended.—**J.Z. Aponyok, 2130 Kohler dr., Davenport, Ia.**

The Black Arm Band In School

I have always thought that one of the chief purposes of any educational system is to encourage free thought and free expression of thought. I was also surprised to discover that mourning for the dead and dying, be they American soldiers, Vietnamese women and children or Viet Cong guerrillas, was considered controversial. —**J.R. Miner, Rout 1, Elliott, Ia.**

Sees No "Clear, Present Danger"

To the Editor:

The board is operating under a theory discarded 30 years ago by the highest court in the land because it was too restrictive. There was no "clear and present danger" but merely a fear of the future. The board did not like expression of opinion not under its control. The arm bands represented a threat to its absolute sovereignty. —**Gary Martin, 669 Thirty-fourth st., Des Moines.**

Arm Band Debate "Pretty Silly"

To the Editor:

There's a "big" argument in Des Moines. While men in Viet Nam are being killed, we, back home, safe from the war, argue about arm bands.

If I thought wearing an arm band would save one life by exposing the Viet Nam issue and helping peace movements, I'd certainly wear it. But the only argument that resulted was over whether arm bands should be permitted in the schools. It's pretty darn silly.—**Craig Kaldenberg, student at Roosevelt High School, 4120 Thirtieth st., Des Moines.**

What Is the First Amendment?

The Constitution, written in 1787, is a set of rules and principles that governs the people of the United States. In 1791 ten *amendments*, or changes, were added to the original Constitution. These ten amendments are called the *Bill of Rights*. They protect the basic rights and liberties of Americans.

Part of the First Amendment guarantees freedom of speech, but that does not mean that people can say anything they want at any time. Freedom of speech does not mean that a person may falsely shout "Fire" in a theater or otherwise cause a panic. Freedom of speech may be limited if it presents a "clear and imminent danger." For example, when members of a crowd, some agreeing and others disagreeing with a highly inflammatory speaker have already threatened violence, freedom of speech may be limited.

The students believed that their right of free speech had been taken away.

What Is the Fourteenth Amendment?

After the Civil War, newly freed slaves often found their rights being taken away by state governments. At that time Americans were protected only if the federal government took away these rights.

In 1868 the Fourteenth Amendment was added to the Constitution. It says in part that states cannot make or enforce laws that limit the rights of citizens as set forth by the Constitution. It makes the federal government responsible for guaranteeing individual rights (such as freedom of speech) against actions of a state.

The students believed that the state of Iowa, under which the school officials operated, had deprived them of their right of free speech.

The Trial

On July 25, 1966, the Des Moines federal district courtroom was packed with curious citizens and supporters for both sides. Cases involving people accused of disobeying the Constitution or its amendments are tried in federal courts in non-jury trials: only a judge listens to the evidence and decides who is right.

The trial is like a contest between two opponents. Each opponent tries to convince the judge that its side is right. Each side presents witnesses whose testimony tends to support its view of the case. All testimony must reasonably relate to the main issue. Generally witnesses cannot give their opinions. The opposing lawyer tries to break down the accuracy of a story or a witness's trustworthiness.

Since it was not a jury trial, the lawyers had already talked with Judge Roy L. Stephenson about the issues in the case. They *waived* (gave up) their right to opening statements because nothing would be stated in the opening that the judge didn't already know.

Dan Johnston, now the lawyer for the students, was twenty-eight years old. He had graduated from law school two years before. He had worked for the state attorney general's office for a year; he had tried only a few cases in court and had never tried a case in federal court. But Johnston was not nervous. Since there was no jury, there was no risk of something happening to prejudice the jury.

Johnston was not against the Vietnam War, but he did believe that the students' right of free speech had been taken away. He also believed they had carefully thought out their ideas. He hoped they would speak confidently on the witness stand.

Plaintiffs' Strategy

In trying to prove that the school board violated the First and Fourteenth Amendment rights of the students, the plaintiffs will try to prove that:

- the students had been denied their right to express their views;
- the armbands had not disturbed teaching or caused disturbances;
- the ban, by singling out these students, discriminated against them.

Defendants' Strategy

In trying to show that school officials did not violate the students' rights, the defendants hope to prove that:

- the armbands created a potentially dangerous situation;
- disturbances did occur;
- the students had other chances in school to exercise free speech;
- the students had been convinced by their parents to wear the armbands;
- school officials acted reasonably to protect education for all students.

Who Took Part in *Tinker vs. Des Moines?*

Judge Roy L. Stephenson

Clerk

Witness Stand

DEFENDANTS
Allan A. Herrick
Philip C. Lovrien

PLAINTIFFS
Dan Johnston

Witnesses for the Plaintiffs

Witness: John Frederick Tinker

The first witness was fifteen-year-old John Tinker, an eleventh grader at North High School. John was influenced by Quaker beliefs. Every Sunday morning he went to the Quaker meetinghouse for their service and then attended a youth group at the Unitarian Church. Most Quakers do not believe in violence; they do not believe in taking up arms against others. Many Quakers were active in the anti-Vietnam War movement. At the Unitarian youth group the teenagers talked about social justice, the war in Vietnam, race relations, and religious philosophy.

Direct Examination by the Plaintiffs

On the stand John explained how he had come to wear an armband.

Q. Why did you decide to wear a black armband?

A. Well, on Wednesday night, December 15, 1965, Ross Peterson and Bruce Clark came to my house. I know them from a group at the Unitarian Church. They gave me a copy of a document called "We Mourn." I read it and agreed with it. It said:

ATTENTION STUDENTS!

Some high school and college students in Iowa who are interested in expressing their grief over the deaths of soldiers and civilians in Vietnam will fast on Thursday, December 16. They will also wear black arm bands starting that same day. The National Liberation Front (Vietcong) recently proposed a 12-hour truce on Christmas Eve. The United States has not yet replied to their offer. However, [New York] Senator Robert Kennedy has suggested that the truce be extended indefinitely pending negotiations. If the United States takes this action the arm bands will be removed. If it does not the bands will be worn throughout the holiday season and there will be a second fast on New Year's Day. High school and college students are also encouraged to forgo their usual New Year's Eve activities and meet together [at Bruce Clark's home] to discuss this complex war and possible ways of ending the killing of Vietnamese and Americans. . . .

PLEASE COME!

John explained:

The idea of an indefinite truce was Senator Robert Kennedy's. I hoped this truce would stop the killing and might lead to a peaceful settlement in the war.

Bruce and Ross talked with my parents. My sister Mary Beth and I decided to wear armbands. I also decided to fast on both days.

John felt confident that he had done the right thing in wearing the armband to school, but he felt a little nervous as he spoke. He looked around at his friends in the courtroom and he felt less nervous.

John's parents were antiwar activists. John and his mother had been among the sixty Iowans at the November 1965 antiwar demonstration in Washington, D.C. Dan Johnston wanted the judge to understand that although John's family often agreed with his ideas, he had his own independent thoughts.

Q. Do you talk about the war in Vietnam at home?
A. Quite often. I talk about war and peace with my parents and most of my brothers and sisters, although I don't agree with all my parents' views.

Q. Do you feel strongly about these differences with your parents?

A. I don't know what you mean. I wouldn't slug them in the mouth.

The plaintiffs showed that the students were not intentionally defiant; they had tried to talk to school officials before they broke the rule.

Q. When did you wear the armband?

A. I didn't wear mine until Friday, December 17.

John Tinker and his homeroom class

On Wednesday night I learned the principals were opposed. So I didn't wear the armband on Thursday. I didn't feel that I should just wear it without trying to talk to the school board first, but most of the kids wore theirs on Thursday. Thursday night we called Mr. Niffenegger, the president of the school board, and asked for an emergency meeting with the board, but he turned us down. So some of the kids, including me, decided to wear the armbands the next day.

On Friday, December 17, John wore a tie, white shirt, and jacket to school. He didn't usually dress this formally for school, but he didn't want to be criticized for being badly dressed that day. The war was a serious matter to him, and he wanted to be taken seriously. For the first half of the day he wore the armband on the left sleeve of his jacket. When he realized that it didn't stand out enough on his dark jacket, he took off his jacket and pinned it to his white shirt.

He described his day in school, hoping to prove that his armband had not provoked any trouble.

Q. Tell us what happened on December 17.
A. Well, I arrived in school around 7:30 A.M. for orchestra. I was almost late, so I didn't have time to put the armband on. I put it on in the boys' rest room, after homeroom, about 8:30 A.M.

Next was drama class with Mr. Thompson. I'm not sure he saw me wearing it. He didn't say anything. We were working in groups on a play. He was out of the room much of the time. I felt self-conscious, like I stuck out. Some students asked why I was wearing the armband. I told them why. Some of them didn't think I should do this. I guess they thought it was anti-American or something. But

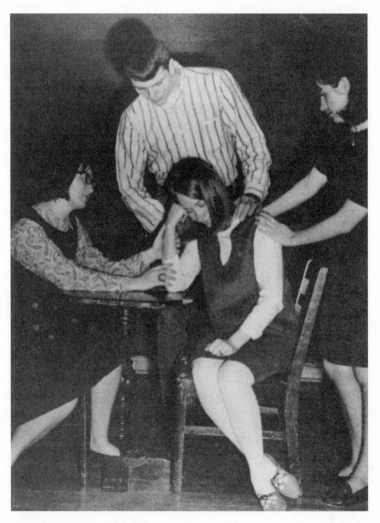

Students in drama class

they thought I should have the right to do it if I wanted to. We talked about it on and off during the class.

At 10:30 I went to algebra with Mr. Worden. I

don't believe he saw it. He said nothing about it. I sit in the back of the class and I don't think anybody saw it. I didn't wear it with my gym clothes, so there was no talk of it during gym, but there was some talk before. After gym, in the locker room, some students made fun of me. Some of my friends said they didn't want me to get in trouble. For about four minutes two or three boys made unfriendly remarks.

The plaintiffs wanted to prove that the armband had not caused any disruption or created a dangerous situation.

Q. Did anyone threaten you with physical harm?
A. No. At lunch some students I often eat with warned me in a friendly manner to take the armband off. For about ten minutes, some kid I had had a feud with in the seventh grade made smart remarks. There were four or five people with him. There were quite a few other students standing around. A football player named Joe Thompson told the kids to leave me alone, that everybody had their own opinions.

Q. Were you afraid you might be hit?
A. At no time was I in fear that they might attack me or hit me. There were too many people around. There were faculty members and school staff people there most of the time. None of them entered into any of this.

Q. What about the rest of your day?

A. After lunch I went to English with Mr. Lory. As soon as I walked into his room, he told me to go to the principal's office. I called my parents before I got there. They had told me to call if anything went wrong or if I got in trouble. I reached my father.

Then I went to see Mr. Wetter, the principal. He said, "I suppose you know I have to ask you to take it off." And I said, "Yes, I do." He said, "I don't suppose you will," or something like that. And I said, "No." I can't remember exactly what he said.

Q. Did he tell you why you couldn't wear it?

A. He said that he was following orders from higher up. I told him I wasn't going to take it off. He told me I would have to leave school, but I wouldn't be suspended and it wouldn't go on my record. He said that as soon as I took the armband off, or as soon as there was a different rule about it, I could come back.

Q. Did he say anything else?

A. He said for his own personal reasons he wanted to know why I was wearing it. So I told him. I guess he was in World War II, because he told me about that.

John's father, Leonard Tinker, came to school and talked with the principal. John was not officially suspended, but he was told he could not come back to school wearing the armband until the rule was changed.

Cross-Examination by the Defendants

Seventy-year-old Allan A. Herrick, one of the lawyers for the school board, was a partner in one of Des Moines's largest law firms. Most of his legal work was for insurance companies. He had never tried a case involving constitutional law. Herrick hoped to show that it was not the students' idea to wear the armbands; they had been influenced to wear them by their parents.*

Q. Were your parents present when Ross and Bruce came to see you?

A. Yes.

Q. And what decision did all of you make that night?

A. I didn't make any definite decision that night.

Q. Four days before, on Saturday, December 11, there was a meeting at the Eckhardts'. Did your mother attend that meeting?

A. I'm not sure. She could have.

Q. Well, did she discuss at home what was talked about during that meeting?

A. I can't remember. I really can't.

Q. Well, what I'm getting at, John, is this business of wearing armbands didn't just come to you like a

---

*Herrick is no longer alive, and the newspapers provided no information on how he felt during the trial.

bolt out of the blue on Wednesday night when Ross came by, did it?

Herrick's tone was somewhat angry, but John didn't feel he was being personally attacked.

A. The idea came from some earlier meetings. But I learned the details from Bruce and Ross on Wednesday night.

Q. Had the armband demonstration been talked about by your mother or father?

A. I can't remember talking about it in my family before Wednesday night.

Q. You have participated in several other demonstrations against the Vietnam War. Were your parents in these demonstrations too?

A. I suppose, most of them.

Q. Who was at the meeting Thursday night, December 16?

A. Students who had worn the armbands that day and other interested people. My sister was there. So was Chris Eckhardt, Chris Singer, Ross Peterson, and Bruce Clark, and some others whose names I do not know. Bruce hadn't worn an armband. He wore a black suit to school. Chris Singer had worn an armband, and she had been sent home from school.

Q. What did you talk about at the meeting?

A. What had happened at school. Then Ross or Bruce called Mr. Niffenegger, the president of the school board. We asked him if we could talk with him before the regular board meeting on Tuesday, December 21. We thought that if the board knew what had happened that they would change their decision. He said he would not call a special meeting. You see, Christmas vacation was starting on Wednesday, December 22, so if we didn't get a special meeting and get permission we would have only one day to wear the armbands and we didn't think that was quite long enough.

Herrick pointed out that the school policy did not deprive students of free speech outside the school.

Q. Did this rule forbid you from wearing armbands outside school?

A. No, but I wanted to be able to wear the armband to school, because I didn't see anything wrong with it. In fact, I thought it was kind of good. That's why I was going to wear it. I wanted to wear it as many days in school as I could.

The defendants pressed John to admit that he had deliberately broken a rule.

Q. So even though you knew about the rule, you wore the armband?

A. Let me try to explain. I didn't wear it Thursday because we were still trying to get hold of Mr. Niffenegger to talk with him. But when I read the newspaper Friday morning, and—I don't know—it could have been hearsay, but the paper said something to the effect that there wouldn't be any meeting. I believe the word *trivial* was mentioned in it. That it was all a trivial matter. Somewhere along the line Mr. Niffenegger gave that indication. And I thought—you know—he could at least listen to us—I don't know—I guess then I decided to wear it.

The defendants wanted to show that the armband had attracted attention and was potentially explosive.

Q. Were any remarks made to you about the armband?

A. Yes. Some of my friends made complimentary remarks and those who weren't my friends made uncomplimentary remarks.

Q. Were there some minor disturbances at lunch?

A. Yes. Some students made uncomplimentary remarks. Some referred to me as a "Commie" and other things like that. Then this one boy quieted everything down and told everybody to lay off me.

Q. So did you attract attention wearing the arm-band?

A. I was attracting some.

Q. And that's what you wanted to do, isn't it?

A. Well, I didn't want to go out with a banner say-ing, "Here I am," if that's what you mean. But I did hope that students would see my armband, and I welcomed any questions about why I was wearing it.

Redirect Examination by the Plaintiffs

The plaintiffs wanted to show how serious John's feelings against the Vietnam War were.

Q. You said that you believed the school board president considered this a trivial matter. How did that make you feel?

A. I do not consider this a trivial matter. It is important to me because I morally think it is wrong. When people are getting killed, that's important to me.

The plaintiffs emphasized John's independent decision to wear the armband.

Q. Was wearing the armband your idea or your parents?

A. Mine. These views were not imposed upon me by my parents. I like to think that I thought it out myself. At first my father opposed my wearing the armband, but my mother didn't. I can't remember the exact reasons why my father opposed it, but I suppose it was because he felt that it would be defying the board, and he didn't think I ought to do that.

The plaintiffs pointed out that the armbands did not cause any more arguments than usually occurred in school.

Q. Do students ever have arguments in the lunch room?

A. Yes. I've heard arguments there on other occasions.

Be the Judge

Does John seem capable of deciding by himself to wear the armband?

Is a silent activity like wearing an armband considered free speech?

Did anything happen to disrupt teaching?

Could any of John's interactions with other students have led to danger?

Witness: **Mary Elizabeth Tinker**

Thirteen-year-old Mary Beth Tinker was an eighth grader at Warren Harding Junior High School. Like her brother John, she attended the Friends Meeting and had been at several anti-war demonstrations with her parents.

In the last year, since the suspension, her family had been threatened several times. Buckets of red paint had been thrown at the front window of their house. On Christmas Eve in 1965 someone telephoned and said the house would be blown up by morning. A few weeks later, when Mary Beth was getting ready for school one morning, the phone rang. A woman asked for her. When Mary Beth got on the phone, the woman said, "I'm going to kill you." One night a radio talk-show host who supported the Vietnam War said that if anyone wanted to go after Mr. Tinker with a shotgun, he would pay the court costs if anything happened.

Direct Examination by the Plaintiffs

Mary Beth felt nervous on the witness stand. It was hard speaking in front of everyone, challenging the people who ran her school. She testified that she had started thinking seriously about war and peace when she was in the fourth grade. She said she often talked about these subjects with her parents, but they had not influenced or convinced her to wear an armband.

Mary Beth's armband was a strip of black cloth about one inch wide pinned on her left arm over her black sweater. She had worn it on Thursday, the day before John wore his. The plaintiffs showed that nothing had happened to her that day other than the normal talking or teasing among students.

Q. What happened on December 16?
A. I arrived in school at 8:00 A.M. for chorus, but no one noticed the armband until science, when the girl next to me asked about it. I told her why I was wearing it. I had a petition saying that we should have the right to wear armbands or crucifixes or

anything like that. She signed it. One other girl talked to me and signed it too. That was about all the talk of it in that class.

In homemaking, the teacher, Mrs. Bell, pointed to the armband. I saw the other students look at it. A couple of kids who sat at my table told me I had better take it off or I would get in a lot of trouble. I told them I was going to wear it.

Q. Is it unusual for girls in homemaking to talk?

A. No. Everyone talks while we sew.

Q. Were they threatening you?

A. No, they just wanted to keep me out of trouble.

Q. Were there other reactions that day?

A. The boy who sits behind me in history kept telling me I'd better not wear it because I would get into trouble. Going to English class, some students told me that I had better take it off. The teacher didn't mention it, nor did anyone else in English.

At lunch a couple of girls at my table told me I had better take it off or some teachers would get me in trouble. A table of boys sitting behind us sort of made some smart remarks. They were just teasing. They always do that to us, about anything. They started saying they wanted black armbands for Christmas, but they didn't think they would be able to get any.

Q. Do students often talk between the lunch tables?

A. Yes, lots of times.

Q. Have you ever seen a teacher stop kids from dis-
cussing things in the cafeteria?

A. There's a teacher in the lunch room, and lots of
times, when the boys are bothering us, she gives
them passes to go to the office and stay after school.

Q. What happened after lunch?

A. I went back to the second half of English. No-
body said anything. Then I went to Mr. Moberly's
math class. The day before, we had spent the whole
time talking about student protests. Mr. Moberly
said he didn't like student protests because the students didn't have anything better to offer. He said
that if anyone demonstrated in his class they would
get kicked out. I asked him if he would consider
wearing a black armband a demonstration, and he
said yes.

I walked in and sat down in the back of the
room. Mr. Moberly stands in the back until the bell
rings. He walked by my desk and put a pass to Mrs.
Tarmann's office on my desk. I picked up my books
and went to Mrs. Tarmann's office. She wasn't in, so
I sat down and waited for her. Mr. Willadsen, the
boys' advisor, came in and asked me why I was in the
office. I told him I wasn't sure but I thought it was
because of my armband. He told me that all I had to
do was to take it off. So I took it off and gave it to
him. Then he gave me a pass to go back to math.

I was in math class about ten minutes when I

was called back to Mrs. Tarmann's office. She told me she was sorry but she would have to suspend me. She said she had to follow orders, but she sympathized with my opinion. She told me she understood my point of view because her grandparents had been Quakers. She gave me a notice that says you have been suspended. I had never been suspended before. She told me my parents had to sign it and bring it back before I returned to school.

Be the Judge

Did the armband distract students?

Did Mary Beth's armband disrupt or stop teaching in any of her classes?

Could the teasing at lunch have led to something serious?

Cross-Examination by the Defendants

Again the defendants tried to show that Mary Beth's parents and other adults had initiated the demonstration.

Q. Did any of your other brothers or sisters, aside from John, wear armbands that day?
A. Paul and Hope also wore them. Paul is eight. Hope is eleven.
Q. Did your parents tell them why they were wearing the armbands?
A. My parents didn't have to explain; they understood perfectly well.
Q. Who put the armbands on the little ones?
A. I don't remember. Whoever they asked to.
Q. Who bought the ribbon for the armbands?
A. My mother bought it after we decided to wear the armbands.

The defendants pointed out that though armbands were banned in school, Mary Beth had freedom of expression in her classes.

Q. What did you talk about in Mr. Moberly's class?
A. Well, the principals' ban on armbands started the talk. Mr. Moberly talked about student protests and said that students just protested to be doing something. I don't think he specified any particular protests. Not many students talked. I asked Mr.

Moberly a few questions. I asked him if he considered wearing a black armband a demonstration and he said yes, and that whoever wore one would be kicked out of his class.

Redirect by the Plaintiffs

The redirect clarified that Mr. Moberly, not Mary Beth, had interrupted the teaching.

Q. How much of math was taken up by this talk?
A. The whole period.
Q. Did Mr. Moberly try to stop it or change the subject back to math?
A. No. I think he started it. And he did most of the talking. I was the only student who disagreed with his views.

Be the Judge

Does Mary Beth seem capable of thinking this decision through by herself?

Could eight-year-old Paul Tinker really understand what the armbands meant? Did he wear his because Mary Beth and John were wearing them?

Did Mr. Moberly disrupt education by talking about student protests?

Witness: **Christopher Paul Eckhardt**

Direct Examination by the Plaintiffs

Sixteen-year-old Chris was a sophomore at Theodore Roosevelt High School. He also belonged to the youth group at the Unitarian Church. Chris's parents, like the Tinkers, were antiwar activists. His mother was the president of the Des Moines chapter of the Women's International League for Peace and Freedom. Chris's testimony probed his decision to wear the armband.

Q. How did you learn about the demonstration?

A. My parents told me. They learned about it at a meeting at our house on Saturday afternoon, December 11. I didn't go to the meeting. It sounded like a nice thing to do, but I didn't decide right away that I would do it. I thought about it for a few days, and then on Wednesday night, December 15, I told them I was going to do it.

Chris wore his armband over a cocoa-brown jacket on Thursday, December 16. He was suspended before he went to his first class.

Q. Why did you go directly to see the principal?

A. Well, the morning paper said that the principals had banned the armbands. I thought I might be suspended, so I went directly to see the principal. He was in a meeting. I waited about 45 minutes. Then I saw Mr. Blackman, the vice principal. He looked at my armband and asked me which teacher had asked me to take the armband off. I told him no one. So he asked me to take it off. I told him I wasn't going to do that. I think he said he would have to suspend me

if I didn't because there was a rule against it.

We talked awhile, and then he called my mother and told her that he was going to have to suspend me. He asked me to remove my armband a couple

more times. We talked a little while longer—I can't remember exactly what about—and then Mrs. Cross, the girls' advisor, came in. Mr. Blackman shut the door and told her, "We have a student here wearing a black armband and he doesn't want to remove it."

Mrs. Cross sat down beside me. She said this was going to look bad on my record. Before that Mr. Blackman had told me that I had a good school record and asked if I was looking for a busted nose. I told him I wasn't, and he said something like, "How is your suspension going to look on your record?" Mrs. Cross informed me that the colleges didn't accept demonstrators or protesters. Then they asked me to remove it again. I told them I was going to keep it on. Mr. Blackman gave me a pass to go home. The pass said I would get all fives for the classes that I missed. Five is an F. Same as failing. Mr. Blackman also told me that a suspension notice would come in the mail.

In the middle of Chris's testimony in court, Mr. Blackman got up from his seat and left the courtroom.

The plaintiffs believed that the real reason for banning the armbands was that school officials objected to the students' antiwar views.

Q. Did either Mrs. Cross or Mr. Blackman say what they thought of your views?

A. I can't remember, but they said something like I could wear the armband before and after school if I wanted to. I think Mrs. Cross asked me how old I was and I told her. She said that she thought I was too young and immature to have too many views, and that I ought to take the armband off. They let me know that while I was suspended, that I could probably have plenty of time to look for a new school to go to. I told them I liked Roosevelt and I wanted to come back. They said that if I did anything like this again, I wouldn't come back.

Q. Did they say anything about how your wearing the armband would affect the school?

A. Well, only that it was going to make the school look bad because there would be lots of bad publicity for the school.

Q. Was there any violence or threat of violence that week?

A. Well, Bruce and Ross didn't wear armbands to school on Thursday. They wore black suits. When they went to eat lunch near the shopping center near school, there was some kid there who didn't go to Roosevelt. I don't know his name. He had attended Roosevelt and was kicked out. He pushed them or something like that.

Chris was suspended from school. His grades were not affected by the days he was out of school.

DES MOINES PUBLIC SCHOOLS

NOTICE OF SUSPENSION

To Mr. and Mrs. William Eckhardt   Date December 16, 1965

Address 3818 Lanewood Drive   Regarding: Christopher Eckhardt
                                              (Parent or Pupil)

From Roosevelt High School   Birth Date April 29, 1950   Grade 10
          (School)

This is to inform you that Christopher Eckhardt
has been suspended from school because: of his refusal to comply with school request.

It will be necessary for a parent or guardian to call Mr. Don Blackman

of Roosevelt High School - Call Dec. 20   Telephone number 255-2155
for an appointment.

(Signed) _____
          Vice (Principal)

Form 683   200 pads   6-64   D. M. Tech Press

Cross-Examination by the Defendants

The defendants aimed to show that Chris deliberately broke the school rule.

Q. Why did you go directly to the office?
A. Because I knew I was breaking a rule. I didn't expect exactly to be suspended. But I wanted to tell them I had the armband on, and I intended to wear it. I didn't know exactly what they would do.
Q. Did you expect the principal to make an exception in your case?
A. I didn't know exactly what he would do. The idea of suspension was in my mind.

Chris, Mary Beth, and John returned to school on January 4. They wore all black for the next few months. Black is the color of mourning.

Be the Judge

Were Mrs. Cross and Mr. Blackman threatening Chris or were they pointing out how the suspension might affect his future?

Does Chris seem mature enough to have thought out his ideas?

Do students have to agree with rules to follow them?

Witness: **Donald Wetter**
Direct Examination by the Plaintiffs

 Donald Wetter, the principal of John Tinker's school, was named a defendant in the case.

Dan Johnston *subpoenaed* many of the defendants as plaintiff witnesses—he officially ordered them to appear. In a civil case (not involving a crime), defendants must testify if they are called to do so. There were facts that Johnston felt could be better proved by the defendants than by the students. The students did not have firsthand knowledge about these facts.

Q. Why did you see John Tinker on December 17?
A. The rule had come down from a meeting of principals and I had advised the teachers to refer any students wearing black armbands to me.
Q. When that policy was drawn up, had any student worn an armband to school?
A. Not to my knowledge.

Cross-Examination by the Defendants

Most educators consider school officials and teachers as being *in loco parentis*, in place of parents, during the school day. In this role, they have the right and duty to make rules to protect the students' well-being. When students

disobey their rules, officials may punish them as parents punish their children. The school officials believed they were legitimately acting in their role as concerned adult caretakers.

Q. What took place with John in your office?

A. He was wearing a black armband. I asked him if he knew about the rule against it. He said he did. Then I told him that I would ask him to remove the armband. If he refused, my duty was to call his parents and ask one of them to pick him up. He couldn't come back to school until he removed the armband or the policy was changed. I further advised him that this policy had been made with my knowledge and agreement. He explained that the armband was to protest the war and to influence people toward a truce. He said he wouldn't remove it. As I was calling his father, my secretary told me that Mr. Tinker was in the outer office. He came in and I explained the school policy to him. I said that John would not be formally suspended and he could return to school whenever he removed the armband. I also told him that John would not suffer any consequences so far as grades because of this action, and that I would do everything within my power to protect his rights, including his personal welfare.

The defendants wanted to show that the school had shown its concern about the war in a number of school programs.

Q. Did you talk with John about anything else?

A. I reminded him about our Veterans Day school program, when I had expressed my concern about the war dead to the students. I also said that I personally felt that there were appropriate times to mourn our war dead, such as Veterans Day and Memorial Day. I stated that it did not seem appropriate or necessary to me to mourn the war dead as he was doing. I told him I was a veteran of World War II and the Korean War.

Be the Judge

Were school officials against the antiwar views of the students or were they worried about possible disturbances in the school?

Why couldn't the students exercise their right of free speech by talking in an assembly program instead of wearing the armbands?

Witness: **Donald Blackman**

Direct Examination by the Plaintiffs

Mr. Blackman, the vice principal at Theodore Roosevelt High School, was called to the witness stand. He returned to the courtroom.

Q. Did you see Chris Eckhardt on December 16?

A. Yes. He came to my office wearing a black armband. We talked. I told him he was going to be officially suspended because he was breaking a school rule.

Cross-Examination by the Defendants

The defendants wanted to show that the rule was not drawn up because school officials were against the students' antiwar views; the rule came about because school officials felt demonstrations were improper in school and potentially dangerous.

Q. Did you talk with Chris?

A. Yes, I asked him why he was wearing the armband. He explained. Then I told him I wasn't concerned with what he believed in. I was concerned that he had been notified not to wear an armband in school. He hadn't followed the rule, so he was being suspended. I told him that we could not permit demonstrations about different beliefs.

Q. Did anyone else speak to him?

A. Mrs. Cross, the girls' advisor, came in while I was talking to him. She tried to reason with him and get him to remove the armband. His future as far as a record was mentioned because anytime you are suspended, it becomes a matter of record. Colleges ask about students' records, and his suspension would show on his.

Redirect by the Plaintiffs

The plaintiffs, hoping to convince the judge that the rule discriminated against armband wearers, pointed out that other "distracting" or "controversial" symbols had been allowed in school.

Q. Have you ever seen students wearing religious symbols such as Iron Crosses, which are associated with Nazi Germany?
A. I suppose. I haven't really paid much attention.

Q. Do you ever see students wearing political buttons?
A. There probably were political buttons. Frankly I never really noticed.

Q. Was the armband rule the first rule against wearing political or religious symbols in the Des Moines schools?

A. Yes.

Be the Judge

Could wearing Iron Crosses start trouble?

Is wearing a political button expressing a political view? If so, why are buttons allowed and armbands forbidden?

Witness: **E. Raymond Peterson**

Direct Examination by the Plaintiffs

Peterson, the Director of Secondary Education in Des Moines, was at the meeting when the high school principals drew up the rule against armbands. The rule had not been written down. Again the plaintiffs pointed out that the rule was discriminatory because other symbols were allowed in school.

Q. Were there any rules before about political or religious symbols?

A. No. But we never had this kind of situation before.

Q. Was this policy directed only at the students wearing black armbands?

A. Not at the students; at the principles of it. We had no particular students in mind. It was anyone who might go against the rule, any one of the 18,000 students.

Q. Wasn't the rule over the principle of the Vietnam War?

A. No, it was over the principle of the demonstration.

Q. Was the rule specifically about wearing armbands?

A. Yes.

Cross-Examination by the Defendants

Peterson's testimony stressed that the rule was made to avoid trouble, not to squelch the students' views.

Q. Did you say the following to a newspaper reporter? "For the good of the system we don't think the armbands should be permitted. The schools are no place for demonstrations. We allow for free discussion in classes. The decision not to allow students to wear armbands was based on a general school policy against any disturbing situation in the school. We believe that education would be disturbed by students wearing armbands."

A. Yes, I said that.

Q. Is there a school policy about demonstrations in the classroom?

A. It's understood among the principals that anything which interrupts education may be excluded. Now, if it's part of the curriculum, it's a different matter.

Be the Judge

Was education disturbed in any of the three schools?

Witness: **Ora Niffenegger**

Direct Examination by the Plaintiffs

Niffenegger, the president of the Des Moines School board, was also named as a defendant.

Q. When did you learn about this matter?
A. On Thursday, December 16. But the board didn't act on it then. On Tuesday, December 21, we talked about it again, but we didn't reach a decision then either. We decided to wait to learn more and get advice from our lawyer. When we met again at our regular meeting, on January 3, 1966, we voted to uphold the policy.

Cross-Examination by the Defendants

The school officials wanted to show that the board had not ignored the students' request for a special meeting.

Q. Who called you about a special meeting?

A. Four people. The first two were students. They were very courteous. Two women also called. I told the students they should speak with their principals. They told me they had tried this and were turning to me as a last resort. I tried to be nice to them, because all my life, if I may say so, I have worked with young people. I told them that there were several reasons why I couldn't do this. Legally I would have to call each board member to make sure that we would have a majority present. Then I would have to mail each person a written notice. By law, that notice had to be sent 48 hours ahead of time. There just wasn't enough time to do this. I did tell the boys that anyone could speak at the regular board meeting. If they gave me their names ahead of time, we would put them on the agenda if there was time.

Q. Did they say why they wanted to wear the armbands?

A. Yes. The armbands showed their opposition to U.S. policy in Vietnam. I explained the best that I could that I thought they were taking the wrong way out. I said that in our country we had a well-defined way to handle this matter: If they didn't like the way our elected officials were handling things, it should be handled with the ballot box and not in the halls of our public schools.

Niffenegger described the atmosphere at the school board meeting that convinced him that the armbands were an explosive issue.

Q. Was there a demonstration at the school board meeting?

A. Yes. The room was filled to overflowing. There were a few people holding signs. Several times it was very hard to keep order, but we did get through. There were local people at the meeting. And some outsiders.

Q. Were there demonstrators outside the building?

A. I don't know firsthand, but I saw some newspaper photos of people demonstrating outside.

Be the Judge

Was Niffenegger against the armbands because he disapproved of demonstrations?

If outsiders were involved, does that make a difference?

The plaintiffs rested their case.

Witnesses for the Defense

The plaintiffs had called many school officials, all of whom had been cross-examined by the defendants. The defendants felt that their side of the case was clear from these witnesses. So they called only two witnesses.

Witness: Dick Moberly
Direct Examination by the Defendants

Dick Moberly was Mary Beth's math teacher. Mary Beth's father, Leonard Tinker, had also been Mr. Moberly's minister. Moberly greatly respected Reverend Tinker even though he thought that his participation in antiwar demonstrations was wrong. He felt these demonstrations were disrespectful to the American soldiers fighting in Vietnam. The defendants thought that Moberly's testimony would show that freedom of expression was encouraged in the Des Moines schools.

Q. Did you talk with your students about arm-bands?

A. Yes, on December 15. But it wasn't on armbands only. It started from a newspaper report about the ban on armbands.

Q. What is this class of students like?

A. They are an exceptional group. They have good minds and are very sharp. They ask a lot of questions, and sometimes these questions are other than about mathematics. But I feel I should try to answer them as they come up.

Q. Did you spend a lot of time talking in class?

A. Probably five or ten minutes. The talk dragged on to different demonstrations going on in the country then. We could have spent as long as thirty minutes on it. I believe it kind of wrecked the class, but we got through it and had a little time at the end for study and getting ready for the next day's lesson.

Q. What did you say about demonstrations?

A. I ended up by saying if there was going to be a demonstration in class, it should be for or against something in math.

Q. In other words, you wanted them to stick to math?

A. Yes.

Cross-Examination by the Plaintiffs

The plaintiffs believed that Moberly was also prejudiced against student demonstrations.

Q. Did you express your opinion about student demonstrations?

A. I tried to give students a different opinion from what they were getting from the newspaper. I don't believe I tried to give them my opinion, because as a teacher I just try to stimulate their thinking.

Q. What did you say about the armbands?

A. Some students asked, "Was wearing an armband a demonstration?" I said it was. I hadn't really ever thought about it before.

Q. Did you allow this discussion?

A. I believe I was led into it, and continued on with it, and then I cut it off. I should have cut it off sooner. I would rather not get led into discussions like this, but I hate to stop them if students start talking.

Q. Do you think that the more experiences and activities that students have, the more they will benefit from their education?

A. Yes, I would say that. I wouldn't say that it should be in my class only, though. Some of this should be held to other classes. I can't let this go on in my class too often.

The plaintiffs wanted to show that Mary Beth was capable of making up her own mind.

Q. Does Mary Beth have an inquiring sort of mind?

A. She is a very good student and a delight to have in my class.

Q. With or without an armband?

A. With or without an armband.

Q. Has she ever worn anything that disrupted your class?

A. Not that I know of.

The plaintiffs asked again about other symbols worn in school.

Q. Have you ever seen any buttons in school?

A. It has been held to a minimum. I think we have had to run kids to the office when they were running a stream of buttons down their front.

Q. Would one button with a picture of Senator Goldwater or President Johnson on it be objectionable to you?

A. I don't think it would.

Q. Would such a button disrupt your class?
A. I hope not.

Q. Do you think wearing a button with President Johnson on it violates the school rule?
A. I don't know. Any time I have been questioned, I ask my superiors for an interpretation of the rule.
Q. Are you familiar with the Iron Cross?
A. Yes, it's a Nazi symbol. I have seen it worn in my class and I have ridiculed students wearing it. I have told them that they were degrading the country's medals. But I have never kicked them out of class over it.

Q. Is the Iron Cross included in the policy against armbands?
A. Not that I know of.
Q. Have these Iron Crosses ever caused any disruption in your class other than your ridiculing of the students?
A. Not that I know of.

Q. Have you seen Iron Crosses in school since Mary Beth was suspended for wearing an armband?
A. I believe so.

Be the Judge

Why aren't all symbols banned under this school rule?

Witness: **Leonard Tinker**

Leonard Tinker, John and Mary Beth's father, was not in Des Moines the day of the trial, so his deposition was read into the trial record. Depositions are taken before a trial when lawyers are preparing their cases. They are in question-and-answer form like trial testimony.

Tinker was a Methodist minister, but he no longer had a position in a church. He had lost his ministry when black churchgoers wanted to integrate his chuch. Tinker had supported their actions, but the white church members had not. Now he worked for the American Friends Service Committee, an affiliate of the Quakers, as Secretary for Peace Education. He organized conferences for adults and children and he ran a summer camp for families.

The defendants intended to show that Tinker and other adults had planned the armband demonstration and convinced their children to do it.

Q. Do you know what was talked about at the December 11 meeting at the Eckhardt house?

A. I was not part of this meeting. I came at the very end to pick up my wife. But I am generally aware of what took place because they told me.

Q. Do you know of other meetings held about the armband demonstration?

A. There was another meeting at the Eckhardts' home on Sunday, December 12. My children were there.

Q. Did they talk to you about this meeting?

A. After meetings like this, we usually talked about what went on. But my children's interest in wearing the armbands was stimulated by talking to others. They can tell you who.

Q. Did your children talk to you about these armbands?

A. We discussed it before they went to school that morning. By then I knew that the school board had announced the ban, and I raised a very serious objection with the youngsters and with my wife about whether they should wear the armbands, but as I listened to them, I became convinced that this was very definitely a matter of conscience for them. They were not lightly defying authority. They had strong beliefs and they were exercising their constitutional rights. I had to make a choice if I would stand by my children in saying something that I thought was true and honorable. I had either to be with them or not with them. I felt I had to stand with them, and I still do.

The defendants pressed Tinker on his support of his children's "illegal" action.

Q. So you supported their wearing the armbands even though it violated a school policy?

A. I did not ignore that fact. I thought the school officials had to obey the Constitution and I still do. I believe my children have both a right to their conscience and a right to speak. These rights are very important, so I intend to uphold them.

Q. And you felt that that was regardless of the place where they were to express their conscience or their belief?

A. A person's conscience is not restricted to place. Nor, by the way, is the constitutional right of free speech as far as I know.

Q. Do you think you can say anything you want to in a school?

A. No. I don't think I can say anything I want to anywhere. I believe authorities ought to be obeyed but not absolutely always. There are times when authorities must be questioned. It seemed to me this was one of these times.

During the taking of the deposition, the defendants' lawyer, Allan Herrick, kept calling

Tinker a Communist. Johnston repeatedly told Herrick if he didn't stop, Mr. Tinker would not continue answering questions. Herrick eventually stopped calling Tinker a Communist, but the tone of his questioning remained hostile.

Herrick repeatedly asked Tinker about SDS (Students for a Democratic Society). SDS was a controversial group consisting mostly of college students. Many people accused SDS of being Communist led or at least sympathetic to communism. SDS strongly criticized American policy in Vietnam and led many antiwar demonstrations.

Q. The newspaper states that the picket line outside the school board office was made up of members of SDS. Are you familiar with this group, which has been critical of American policy in Vietnam?

A. I am familiar with several organizations I don't run. And many people are critical of U.S. policy in Vietnam.

Q. Didn't SDS direct this demonstration?

A. The students who were suspended from school were not members of SDS. Nor were they directed by SDS, nor were they organized by SDS and they were not following a program of SDS.

Q. But weren't members of SDS present at the meeting when this was talked about?

A. Yes. This group included persons who belong to SDS, but that does not make it an SDS idea.

Be the Judge

What does Tinker mean by saying "A person's conscience is not restricted to place"?

Does it matter if SDS members were at the meeting when the demonstration was being discussed?

The defense rested its case.

After hearing the facts in the case, Judge Stephenson had to decide:

Was the armband a form of speech protected by the First Amendment?

Were the students deprived of their right of free speech?

What do you think the judge decided?

Turn the page to find out.

Judge Stephenson's Opinion

On September 1, 1966, Judge Stephenson issued his written *opinion*. An opinion is the reason for a judge's decision.

He decided in favor of the school officials. He did not think the ban deprived the students of their right of free speech. But he did agree that the armbands were a form of speech. This is what he wrote:

School officials had good reason for the ban. In 1965, the mood in Des Moines and other American cities was explosive. There were arguments everywhere over the Vietnam War. There were draft-card burnings and protest marches. Two draft-card burning cases involving Iowa students were up before this court. The mood at the two school board meetings was heated.

The armbands might not have been disruptive, but other students might have reacted to them and caused disruptions. If school officials reasonably expect a disturbance in the school, they can make rules to prevent it. Unless their rules are unreasonable, the court should not interfere.

The armbands are a form of symbolic speech, but the students' right of free speech was only very slightly limited. They had many other opportunities for free speech. They could wear the armbands off school grounds. They could discuss their views on war in classroom discussions.

The students thought Judge Stephenson was wrong. They appealed to the next highest court, hoping it would *overrule*, or reverse, the lower court's opinion.

THE THREATS IN ARM-BAND CASE ARGUED

Headline from the *Des Moines Sunday Register*

In April 1967 the lawyers for both sides argued their case before three judges from the U.S. Court of Appeals for the Eighth Circuit. The judges did not issue an opinion. On October 15, 1967, the lawyers were invited back to argue before all eight judges in that federal Court of Appeals.

On November 3, 1967, the U.S. Court of Appeals issued its opinion. Four judges agreed with the students, and four agreed with the school officials. When the judges are evenly divided, the lower court's decision is upheld.

The Final Appeal

The students took their case to the U.S. Supreme Court, the highest court in the country. It has the final say on interpreting the Constitution, including its amendments.

Nine justices, chosen by the president and approved by the U.S. Senate, sit on the Supreme

Front row: John Harlan, Hugo Black, Earl Warren, William Douglas, William Brennan. Back row: Abe Fortas, Potter Stewart, Byron White, Thurgood Marshall.

Court. The Constitution does not set any quali-
fications for being a justice, but usually the
justices are lawyers. Often they have been
judges on lower federal courts, or legal scholars. Once justices are approved, they may serve
for the rest of their lives.

The Court officially opens on the first Monday in October and ends in June. During that
time the justices review cases in which citizens
believe their constitutional rights have been violated. The justices have different ideas about
how the Constitution should be interpreted.
Some justices believe it should be interpreted
as the Founding Fathers conceived it. Others
believe the world has greatly changed since
colonial times and the Constitution must re-
spond to today's problems. Any decision re-
quires a majority vote—by at least five of the
nine justices.

Thousands of cases are sent to the Court
each year, but very few are reviewed. No one
but the nine justices is present when they de-
bate whether to hear a case. No written record
is made when they talk.

The Supreme Court decided to review the
Tinker case.

Be the Justice

The justices had to decide whether or not:

- the armband was a form of symbolic speech protected by the First Amendment;
- the armbands had disrupted teaching or caused disturbances;
- school officials had deprived the students of the right of free speech;
- the students were unlawfully suspended for exercising their right of free speech;
- the school board had violated the First and Fourteenth Amendments.

Lawyers for both sides were asked to submit *briefs*, or arguments explaining their positions. In a brief lawyers also *cite* (refer to) judicial decisions that support their ideas and attack judicial decisions that disagree.

The Petitioners' Brief

Since the students petitioned the Court for review of the case, they are called *petitioners*. Their brief emphasized five ideas:

The First Amendment applies to students.

The students cited a 1943 Supreme Court decision that said that under the First and Fourteenth Amendments, students could not be forced to salute the flag:

In 1943 public school students in Virginia were required to salute the flag and say the pledge of allegiance. One student refused. He was a Jehovah's Witness. This religious group considers the flag "an image." Its members are not allowed to "bow down" or "serve" such images. The flag is a symbol. It is a way of communicating an idea. The flag is covered under the First Amendment.

The student was exercising free speech. Free speech must be allowed unless it presents a clear and present danger. Refusing to salute and pledge did not interfere with anyone's rights or create a clear and present danger.

Boards of Education are creatures of the state. These boards must do their work within the limits of the Bill of Rights. The Bill of Rights denies those in power the right to force people to think the same thing. (*West Virginia State Board of Education vs. Barnette*)

The students were unlawfully suspended for exercising their First Amendment rights.

To back up their argument that their silent protest was constitutional, the students cited a 1966 Supreme Court decision supporting a silent protest in a library. The Supreme Court had written:

In March 1964 five young Negro men entered a public library in Clinton, Louisiana. The library was segregated: Negroes were not allowed to use it. Brown, one of the men, requested a book. The librarian told him she did not have the book but would order it for him. Then she asked Brown and the others to leave. To protest the library's segregated policies, Brown sat down and the others stood near him. There was no noise or loud talking. After fifteen minutes, they were thrown out, arrested, and charged with disturbing the peace. They were tried in court and found guilty.

Their arrests violated their right of free speech. They had not disturbed the peace. They were quietly protesting and were exercising their First Amendment right of free speech. (*Brown vs. Louisiana*)

The armbands did not disrupt education or discipline.

The students cited a 1966 federal court of appeals decision because it upheld the rights of Mississippi students to express their views in a similar manner to the Des Moines students:

In 1964 a high school principal in Mississippi banned wearing "freedom buttons" in school. The buttons were part of a voter registration drive. In 1964 Negroes in Mississippi were not allowed to vote. School officials said that the ban was a "reasonable" way to keep discipline. Forty students wore the buttons and were suspended.

These buttons were a way of silently communicating the idea that other Negroes should exercise their civil rights. Wearing buttons on collars or shirt fronts is certainly not like carrying banners or making speeches, which have no place in the classroom. If discipline had been disturbed, the principal could have forbidden them. But that did not happen. The rule was unreasonable and violated the students' right of free expression. School officials cannot limit a student's free expression when it does not *materially* and *substantially* interfere with school discipline. (*Burnside vs. Byars*)

The ban was unconstitutional.

The students attacked Judge Stephenson's statement that if a disturbance in school was *reasonably* anticipated, reasonable actions to prevent it are allowed.

> Free speech can be limited only if there is evidence of a "clear or imminent" danger arising directly out of the situation. There was no reason to believe the armbands would cause any trouble. They were not that different from other types of expression—political buttons, religious symbols—which were allowed in the school.
>
> Instead of focusing on what actually happened in the school, the District Court focused on the emotional arguments over the Vietnam war in Des Moines. The Court said that while the armbands may not be disruptive, the reactions from other students would likely have disturbed discipline. There is no evidence to back that up.
>
> And what if other students had reacted so hostilely that education was disrupted? School officials must discipline those who react to speech they don't like, not deny students the right to express themselves. We cannot let threats of disorder stop free speech or it could always be destroyed by a small, hostile group.

The ban discriminated against armbands.

Students in Des Moines have worn emblems and symbols to school before. Some students have worn the "Iron Cross," a symbol used in Nazi Germany, and school officials did nothing about it.

Since political symbols had been allowed before and there were no disturbances, there was no reason to believe that the armbands would cause disturbances. So the ban must have been stimulated by the hostility toward the students' views.

School officials singled out these students from other students. They placed special limits on the expression of their views. In doing so, they struck at the very core of what the First Amendment protects—the expression of unpopular views.

The Respondents' Brief

Since the school officials responded to the students' brief, they are called *respondents*. Their brief emphasized five main ideas.

People do not have a constitutional right to protest wherever they please.

School officials cited a Supreme Court Decision that supported the right of state authorities to limit demonstrations.

> In 1966, college students went to jail to protest the arrests of other student protesters. The students claimed they had a right to demonstrate peacefully on jail-house grounds. We do not agree. People do not have a constitutional right to protest or air their views whenever and however and wherever they please. (*Adderly vs. the State of Florida*)

The students had used *Brown vs. Louisiana* to support their right of silent protest. But school officials pointed out that the Supreme Court had decided this case by a slim margin, 5–4. The four judges who had disagreed had filed a dissent explaining why. The school officials quoted from this dissent:

> If these students had a constitutional right to stay in the library over the protest of the librarians who had lawful authority to keep the library orderly for others, that would mean that the Constitution requires librarians to stand helplessly by while protesting groups stage "sit-ins" or "stand-ups" to dramatize their particular views. If one group can take over libraries for one cause, another group will take them over for another cause. The state could become paralyzed over the use of their libraries, and I suppose that the next step could be to paralyze the schools.

School officials insisted that the students' parents had abused the right of free speech.

> The Tinker and Eckhardt families are professional protesters. The armband demonstration was thought up by them and members of the SDS (Students for a Democratic Society) at a meeting at the Eckhardt home. None of the students was at that meeting. Four of the Tinker children wore armbands to school. Were these children really exercising their constitutional rights, or was Reverend Tinker using his children to spread his propoganda into the schools?

School officials did not deprive students of their right of free speech.

School officials believed that the atmosphere in Des Moines in 1965 was so explosive that they were reasonable in thinking that education would have been disturbed by the armbands. They cited a case in which the federal court of appeals upheld a school rule against "freedom buttons":

On Friday, January 29, 1965, thirty Negro Mississippi high school students wore freedom buttons to school. They created a disturbance by noisily talking in the halls when they should have been in class. The principal told them they could not create a disturbance and they had to remove their buttons.

On Monday, February 1, 150 students came to school wearing buttons. They gave out buttons to other students. They pinned buttons on students even when they didn't ask for them. One younger child cried when someone tried to put a button on her. Class instruction was disrupted. The students were forbidden to wear the buttons at school.

The next day 200 students wore buttons. The principal sent them home. As they left school, classes were disturbed by their comments inviting others to join them. One suspended student went into a classroom, ignored the teacher and without permission tried to get another student to leave class. Some students threw buttons back in the building through the windows.

These students totally disregarded the rights of other students. They created disturbances and interfered with education. They caused a complete breakdown in school discipline. Freedom of speech does not mean an absolute right to speak. Each case must be decided on its own facts. There can be abuses of such freedom. (*Blackwell vs. Issaqauena County Board of Education*)

School officials have the right to adopt reasonable rules.

In 1967 the Iowa Supreme Court upheld a school rule preventing married students from participating in extracurricular activities (basketball). The court said that school boards have the important and difficult job of running public schools. To do their job, they may make rules for the pupils. The court must not interfere with these rules unless the rules are unreasonable.

The armband rule was reasonable.

School officials reminded the justices that Judge Stephenson had believed that the atmosphere in Des Moines in 1965 was so explosive that the school officials were reasonable in thinking that education would be disturbed by the armbands. They gave examples to prove that there had been disturbances and acts of physical violence:

Physical violence was inflicted on one suspended student at Roosevelt. Either Bruce Clark or Ross Peterson said somebody had struck him. John Tinker was warned to take the armband off. He said he was not in fear of being attacked because there were too many people there. Boys made smart remarks to Mary Beth Tinker, warning her that she would get in trouble wearing the armband.

No one can accurately judge what might have happened if school officials had not acted so swiftly. But there had been enough similar demonstrations in schools and other places these past few years to make us realize that there could have been serious consequences if the demonstrations had not been stopped almost before they got started.

Be the Justice

Did the parents influence or manipulate the students?

Was there a "clear and present danger" in Des Moines to justify limiting free speech?

Did the armbands materially and substantially interfere with education and discipline?

Why did school officials permit some political symbols and forbid others?

Now you are ready for the final step. You will enter the courtroom, where the lawyers from both sides will *argue* (explain their positions) and answer any remaining questions you might have about the case. Each side is allowed one half hour to talk. Justices may interrupt at any time with questions.

The Oral Argument

The Petitioners' Arguments

Dan Johnston, the lawyer for the students, had argued this case three times before—in the district court and twice before the Court of Appeals for the Eighth Circuit. But this time, standing in front of the nine Supreme Court Justices, he was nervous. This could be one of the most important events of his career—very few lawyers have the opportunity to argue a case before the Supreme Court. Among the justices on the Court was Hugo Black, one of Johnston's heroes and an expert on the First Amendment.

First Johnston reviewed the facts in the case. He insisted there was a great difference between minor events that momentarily distract students and harmful disruptions that interfere with teaching and discipline. Then the justices asked questions.

Q. What if the students had gotten up in class and insisted on talking about the meaning of their armbands?

A. If that happened, we wouldn't be here.

Q. Did the students wear the armbands to express their message to everybody?

A. Yes.

Q. Why didn't they take them off when they went to class?

A. There was no reason to take them off, because they were not disrupting the class.

Q. But they wore the armbands to class to convey a message. They assumed students would see the armbands and understand and think about them. Are you saying when they wore them in class they intended students to think about them outside the class but not inside the class?

A. I am saying that they chose a method of expression that would not be disruptive.

Q. Physically it wouldn't make a noise or cause a commotion. But don't you think it would make some people focus on the armband and the Vietnam War and think about that instead of what they were supposed to be thinking about?

A. I think it might for a few moments have distracted some students, just as many other things do in the classroom.

Q. Things the school has forbidden?

A. Things the school allows. The school does not attempt to regulate all things that might be distracting.

Q. Are you saying that schools may not keep armbands out of classrooms?

A. Yes. I believe school officials must stop those who disrupt a student's right of free speech rather than limit free speech.

Q. What if fistfights broke out? Would the principals have the right then to ban the armbands?

A. You cannot silence the speaker because others are violent. School officials have a duty to move against those causing the disruption rather than take away the First Amendment right of expression. Of course a substantial disruption to the school might justify limiting free expression. But that doesn't apply in this case, because there is no evidence that these armbands caused any disruptions.

Q. So you believe there could be some whispering in the classroom?

A. Yes, no doubt about that. There was talk at lunch in the cafeteria and some talk in the halls. There was some discussion in John Tinker's drama class.

Q. If the evidence shows that wearing the armband substantially interfered with education, would you then say that school officials could take disciplinary action?

A. Yes. But I want to make a distinction between expressing an opinion that might disrupt the class and expressing an opinion that might cause someone else to disrupt the class. I also want to distinguish between expressing an opinion coupled with something like marching in the hallway or standing up in mathematics class and making a speech about the war in Vietnam. I think the Court can prohibit that.

No school officials testified that the armbands caused any disturbances. We believe school officials overreached their power and took away the right of free speech.

This case is not based on whether or not the students' conduct was permissible. It's based on whether the conduct of school officials is permissible.

Q. Doesn't this case get this court pretty deep in the workings of ordinary day-to-day discipline in schools?

A. I don't think it gets you any further than in *West Virginia State Board of Education vs. Barnette*, when the court said that students could not be required to salute the flag.

Q. Do school officials ever have a right to limit individual expression? For example, suppose some child went to school wearing a ridiculous costume that violated a school rule. And this child says "I am wearing this costume because I want to express the very strong belief that I have in the utmost freedom for the individual." Does that child have a constitutionally protected right to her costume?

A. The real question is whether or not the utterance is an expression as guaranteeed by the First Amendment. The district court did agree that the students were expressing views guaranteed by the First Amendment.

Johnston asked to reserve the rest of his time for a rebuttal after the lawyer for the school officials gave the argument. The justices agreed.

The Respondents' Argument

Allan Herrick, the lawyer for the school officials, posed two questions for the justices to think about:

One: Do school officials have to wait until violence and disorder break out, or may they act promptly when they think it may occur?

Two: How far does the court want to go under the First Amendment in reviewing every decision that school officials make that they believe is necessary to maintain order in the classroom?

We believe the ban was reasonable and did not deprive the students of their right of free speech. In other cases, this Court has ruled that freedom of speech, including the right of demonstration, is not an absolute right to be exercised anytime or anyplace. The case of *Adderly vs. the State of Florida* particularly pertinent. The students went from the university to the jail grounds to protest the arrest of students the day before and—

One of the justices interrupted Herrick and moved him back to what happened in Des Moines.

Q. There were several hundred students involved in Florida. How many were involved in Des Moines?
A. Five were suspended for wearing armbands. Two wearing them were not suspended.

Q. So seven students wearing armbands were disrupting 18,000?

A. Yes, but those figures don't reflect the heated atmosphere in Des Moines and other American cities in 1965. We believe the right of free speech or the right of demonstration in schools must be weighed against the right of school officials to make reasonable rules to avoid disturbances. And there had been with John Tinker what I would call disruption. There were one or two boys struck.

Q. Weren't these very same strong arguments about the war going on in every community then?

A. I think that is true, your Honor, but—

Q. Do you think when people argue that's enough reason to stop freedom of speech?

A. Free discussion in the classroom is always permitted and always has been. But the question is whether students can impose on a captive audience when it is known that people are very upset and that the armbands might disrupt the schools.

It seems that the students are saying that school officials are powerless to act until a disruption occurs. We believe that should not be the rule. Sometimes an ounce of prevention is a lot better than a pound of cure.

Q. On that theory, could the school forbid all discussion or demonstrations in political matters?

A. Not at all. But they could forbid where and when these matters would be discussed.

The justices targeted the wearing of other symbols in school.

Q. Suppose the students wore Humphrey for President or Nixon for President buttons in school. Those buttons might be highly controversial or inflammatory in some communities. Could they wear them?

A. I think if students wore a whole row of political buttons it could be disruptive.

Q. Did the students come in with a whole row of armbands?

A. No.

The justices wanted Herrick to pinpoint why school officials believed there was a "clear and present danger."

Q. What evidence is there that the armbands were explosive?

A. Well, at the trial John Tinker testified that for about four or five minutes in the locker room some students made fun of him for wearing the armband. At lunch, some students he ate with warned him to take the armband off. For about ten minutes one student, who was standing around with four or five others, made smart remarks to him. That happened at lunch. We frankly admit that the disruption was very brief. But when disruption is threatened we believe that school officials are entitled to act.

Q. I agree to that. But where is this evidence that shows there was danger of disruption?

A. John Tinker said he attended a meeting where some students told about physical violence having been inflicted on them when wearing the armband. Bruce Clark or Ross Peterson said somebody had struck him.

Q. If the school board knew about any violence, why wasn't it put in evidence for this case? What evidence of disruption did school officials have when they adopted this rule? Is it on paper anyplace?

A. I think, your Honor, that I have stated that an explosive situation existed in the Des Moines schools when the rule was adopted.

Q. And that explosive situation was that they had a march in Washington, D.C.? What other explosive situation existed in Des Moines?

A. A former student of one of our high schools was killed in Vietnam. Some of his friends are still in school. It was felt that any kind of demonstration might become difficult to control.

Q. Do we have a city in this country that hasn't had someone killed in Vietnam?

A. I think not. I don't think it would be an explosive situation in most cases, but it could be.

Q. It could be explosive. Is that your position?

A. Yes, sir.

Q. Do you think the Constitution prevents schools from banning talk, particularly of very emotional subjects, and allows school officials to say that we will only teach things that the school—

A. I think within reason that is true.

Q. Would you say that school officials could pick out one particular issue and say you cannot do this subject but you can do the rest?

A. I would go further than that, your Honor. I would say today if the atmosphere was different, the armbands should be permitted. Our claim is that in 1965 the school officials acted reasonably. The schools are set up to give children an education. Anything that threatens education ought to be forbidden.

Herrick's time was up. The Chief Justice asked Johnston if he wanted to use his remaining time to rebut. He did.

The Rebuttal

Johnston pinpointed what he thought was a crucial issue in the case: Other symbols were worn in these schools, and they were not forbidden. The rule singled out armbands. The rule was censorship by discrimination. Johnson spoke:

Now Mr. Herrick indicated that there was an explosive situation which made this a special circumstance. But I don't believe that the evidence supports that. The reasons the school board gave for establishing the rule are insufficient to limit speech.

Q. Do you think that the state of Iowa cannot bar political discussions in school?

A. I believe it has the power. The whole point of our case is that they have exceeded that power.

Q. But isn't the state really trying to protect the authority that teachers need to run the schools and establish their right to make rules for teaching?

A. I don't read that from the record.

Be the Justice

Now you will meet with the eight other justices to discuss the case.

Here is what you must decide:

Were the students deprived of their constitutional right to free speech?

To decide that, you must also decide:

Are armbands free speech?

Was the ban against the armbands constitutional?

Did the armbands materially and substantially disrupt education and discipline?

When justices decide a case, they often reread the briefs and various lower-court decisions. They may review trial evidence. At any point in your deliberations, you may turn back to clarify information. Look in the Law Clerk's Notes to find the specific things you want to read.

When you have reached your decision, turn the page to see what the U.S. Supreme Court decided.

The Supreme Court's Decision

On February 24, 1969, the court ruled 7–2* in favor of the students. The opinion of the court was written by Justice Abe Fortas.

Wearing the armband was free speech.
It was a symbolic act to publicize the students' objections to the war in Vietnam. This was an action entirely divorced from actually or potentially disruptive conduct.

The First Amendment applies to students.
Students or teachers do not shed their constitutional rights to freedom of speech or expression at the schoolhouse gate. The First Amendment says that Congress may not abridge (limit) the right to free speech. This provision means what it says. A student

*For: Brennan, Douglas, Fortas, Marshall, Stewart, Warren, White.
  Against: Black, Harlan.

has the right of free speech in the classroom, in the cafeteria, on the playing field, and on the campus.

The Fourteenth Amendment applies to students.

The Constitution says that states may not abridge freedom of speech. The Fourteenth Amendment protects citizens against the state and all its creatures—including boards of education. These boards have important, delicate functions but none that they may not perform within the limits of the Bill of Rights.

The school rule banning armbands was unconstitutional.

In a democracy a vague fear of disturbance is not enough to overcome the right to freedom of expression. Any words spoken—in class, in the lunchroom, or on the campus—may start an argument or cause a disturbance. Our Constitution says we must take this risk. This sort of hazardous freedom—this openness—is the basis of our national strength and of the independence and vigor of Americans who grow up and live in this often argumentative society.

For school officials to forbid a particular form of opinion, their action must be caused by something more than a mere desire to avoid the discomfort and unpleasantness that always accompany an unpopular idea. The forbidden conduct must "materially and substantially" interfere with discipline and education or it cannot be stopped. There is no evidence that school officials had reason to anticipate that the armbands would substantially interfere with education or impinge on the rights of other students. Even the official memo of reasons for the ban did not list disruption as a reason.

The ban appears to have been based on an urgent wish to avoid controversy which might have resulted from the students' silent opposition to the war in Vietnam. It is revealing that the school principals drew up the rule in response to a student telling a journalism teacher that he wanted to publish an article on Vietnam in the school paper. The student was told that the principals were opposed to publishing his article.

It is also relevant that school officials did not forbid all symbols of political or controversial significance but singled out a particular symbol—black armbands worn to express opposition to our nation's involvement in Vietnam.

School officials do not have absolute authority over students.

Students in school and out of school are "persons" under our Constitution. They have fundamental rights which the state must respect, just as the students must respect their duties to the state. Without specific constitutionally valid reasons, school officials must not abridge the right of the students to express their views.

Judge Hugo Black's Dissent

Not all the judges agreed with the majority opinion. Justice Hugo Black explained why he disagreed:

I have always believed that under the First and Fourteenth Amendments neither the State nor the Federal Government has any authority to regulate or censor the content of speech. But I have never believed that any person has a right to give speeches or engage in demonstrations where he pleases and when he pleases.

None of the armband students shouted, used profane language, or were violent in any manner. But their armbands caused other students to poke fun at them. There were warnings and comments. An older football player warned other students to let John Tinker alone. A teacher of mathematics had his class practically "wrecked" by disputes with Mary Beth Tinker. The armbands did divert students' minds from their regular lessons.

While the absence of obscene remarks or loud disorder perhaps justifies the Court's view that the armband students did not actually "disrupt" education, I think the evidence overwhelmingly shows that the armbands did exactly what school officials thought they would—take the students' minds off their classwork and divert them to thoughts about the highly emotional subject of the Vietnam War.

Teachers in public schools are hired to teach there. They are not paid to teach subjects not part of the State curriculum. Nor are students sent to schools to broadcast political or other views. Taxpayers send children to school because at their age they need to learn, not teach. One does not have to be a prophet to know that after this decision today some students in Iowa schools and indeed in all schools will be ready, able, and willing to defy their teachers on practically all orders. This is more unfortunate for the schools since groups of students all over the land are already running loose, conducting break-ins, sit-ins, lie-ins and smash-ins.

I disclaim that the federal Constitution compels teachers, parents, and elected school officials to surrender control of the American public school system to public school students.

Twenty-seven Years Later

ROUNDUP

THEODORE ROOSEVELT HIGH SCHOOL DES MOINES, IA. 50312 MAY 7, 1992 VOLUME 69 NUMBER 15

Free speech rebels return home tonight

Anne Willits

Is it legal for the administration to keep students from wearing hats? Can the assembly committee censor

appealed to the U.S. Supreme Court. The court decided by a 7-2 vote that it was the students' right to wear the armbands because they were essentially practicing free speech, a First Amendment right.

At the time of the suspension, Eckhardt attended TRHS, John Tinker attended North High School, and Mary Beth

high school."

Incidents occur all the time which keep bringing the Tinker case back into the spotlight. In 1984, TRHS senior Scott Haupert exercised his rights by refusing to surrender film of Vice Principal Richard Vignaroli and a policeman at the scene of the annual Homecoming TP extravaganza.

TRHS reacts peacefully to chaos in LA

Emily Selden

On May 8, 1992, John Tinker, Mary Beth Tinker, Christopher Eckhardt, and Dan Johnston were invited to Roosevelt High School to share their memories and feelings about *Tinker vs. Des Moines* with alumni and students.

John Tinker, Lorena Tinker, Dan Johnston, Marjorie Eckhardt, Chris Eckhardt, Mary Beth Tinker

The three former students; Mary Grefe, who was a member of the school board in 1965; and Richard K. Moberly—Mary Beth's math teacher—agreed to be interviewed for this book.

Chris with his parents

Chris Eckhardt graduated from Roosevelt High School and went to Mankato University. For ten years he was a child counselor. Now he works as a supervisor in child-support enforcement: He tracks down parents who don't pay their family support, and establishes paternity to get payments for children.

How did you feel after the Supreme Court decision?

I was in my dorm room at Mankato. I was a sophomore. A reporter called with the news. I was ecstatic. It was a proud day in America for the First Amendment.

What would you say to young people today about freedom of speech?

It is a fundamental principle that our country was

founded on, and we need to foster support for it and defend it.

What did you learn about the U.S. legal system through this experience?

That it works; that if the cause is just, you can use the system and help make a better society.

Would you do the same thing today?

Definitely.

How did this experience affect your life?

I learned to pursue issues I think are just. When I turned eighteen and was eligible for the army, I became a conscientious objector (C.O.) based on moral and ethical grounds. That year, we had a lottery in the U.S. You were called into the army if your number came up. I got lottery #191. The highest number they called in Iowa was 190. So the local draft board asked me to drop my petition to be a C.O., since I wasn't going to be called up anyway. I told them no. I wanted to go on the record as being a C.O. I was denied C.O. status. I appealed to the state draft board, and they voted 3–1 in my favor. I'm still an activist. I was a union vice president in one local and won back an employee's job because he was denied due process, which I understood from our case.

Mary Grefe, a former history teacher at Theodore Roosevelt High School, was on the school board and voted to uphold the ban. She was against the war but had conflicting feelings about the armband protest. She believes "protest has its place at the beginning of a movement. The black marches were necessary to make people aware of segregation. Once people learn the facts, protest loses its impact. We can better protest by being more selective about people we vote for."

Today Grefe teaches leadership skills to groups and individuals and is still active in public service.

How did you feel after the Supreme Court decision?

It didn't really affect me one way or the other. I didn't ever feel intense about it. I didn't believe I had been corrected or chastised by anyone. Being married to a lawyer, I have learned that it's every citizen's right to have his or her grievances heard and addressed. The students had that right.

What would you say to young people today about freedom of speech?

Freedom of speech carries as much a responsibility as a privilege. Calling each other ethnic names is not freedom of speech. You need to think about what you say and its impact on someone else.

What did you learn about the U.S. legal system through this experience?

While I respect the judicial system and the Supreme Court, I think that in a way it is politicized, and therefore a Supreme Court ruling may not necessarily reflect the majority of public opinion. We see that when the Court reverses itself.

Would you do the same thing today?

No. I would try to get the students, teachers, principal, school board members together before the situation got too polarized. Everyone's point of view would be heard so we could produce a satisfactory compromise agreement. Not 100% satisfactory to everyone, but something we could all live with.

Dick Moberly is now chair of the Mathematics Department at North High School. He has taught for 35 years in Des Moines. After the trial he received a letter from Justice Hugo Black. Black wrote that he was sorry that Moberly's math class was interrupted by a social studies question. Black didn't feel the topic was appropriate for math class.

How did you feel after the Supreme Court decision?

I gave Leonard Tinker a buck as a symbolic representation that he had won. I didn't feel any pain or sorrow that I had lost anything. But I didn't like what the decision created: As time went on, we lost the ability to offset other potentially troublesome situations. For example, in the late 1960s we had near black-white riots outside North High. But we couldn't stop the vocal opinion of people I felt were causing trouble.

What would you say to young people today about freedom of speech?

You have a right to express your opinion but no right to belittle or degrade people publicly. I want freedom of speech with responsibility. How to curb it to protect innocent people is difficult.

What did you learn about the U.S. legal system through this experience?

Nothing that I didn't know before. But I was dumbfounded the day I was called into the principal's office and served a paper by a federal officer. According to the law, since I was named as a defendant in the case, I couldn't leave the state without the Court's permission. I felt locked into my state, sort of under house arrest.

Would you do the same thing today?

If the district had the rule, I would follow it.

How did this experience affect your life?

It didn't. At the time I didn't think the issue of the armbands was important enough to end up in court. Looking at it as lawyers and historians do, I see it was more important than I realized then.

John Tinker graduated from North High and attended the University of Iowa for two years. Today he is a computer programmer. John is involved in PeaceParts, a group that sends material aid—such as bicycles, tools, typewriters—to Nicaragua.

How did you feel after the Supreme Court decision?

I felt very happy, because we had been in it for a long time and had lost twice, and then we finally won. I felt from the start that we were right, and it felt good to have the Supreme Court agree.

There were two issues in this case—free speech and the war in Vietnam. We could not pursue the legality of the war in the courts, and this frustrated us. The war continued for ten more years, and that was a horrible experience for us. But to win our case was a victory.

What would you say to young people today about freedom of speech?

Freedom of speech is very important, and it's equally important to think about what you have to say.

What did you learn about the U.S. legal system through this experience?

I learned a lot about its mechanics. I learned that some of the justices are profound thinkers. I have a lot of respect for our legal system, but I recognize it's not perfect. We won our case, but I think there are many good cases that lose. Pursuing change through the legal system can work, but it's not perfect, so people should pay attention to whether our governmental system is working, and use it where it is working.

Would you do the same thing today?

I hope so. It was a hard decision then. It took a lot of courage to do something that made me stick out. Sometimes when I'm faced with tough decisions now, I don't always do what I really think is right. It's hard to make good conscientious decisions.

How did this experience affect your life?

It's difficult to know what my life would have been like without this. I'm proud of my involvement with the case. It's given me an opportunity to meet a lot of people. People often introduce themselves to me and say, "You don't know me, but I know about your case." It's given me the belief that a person has the ability to affect the world.

Mary Beth and her son, Lenny

Mary Beth Tinker graduated from Warren Harding Junior High School and attended North High School for one and a half years. Then her family moved to St. Louis, where she completed high school. She worked part-time and went to college part-time to study nursing. Today she is a nurse and takes care of adults and children. She has a twelve-year-old son named Lenny.

How did you feel after the Supreme Court decision?

Happy and excited.

What would you say to young people today about freedom of speech?

Freedom of speech is something that we will always have to fight for, and there will be those who will want to silence others. Freedom of speech is an issue every day; you work for it every day in small conversations you might have with your friends or in a speech you might make on a political issue.

What did you learn about the U.S. legal system through this experience?

I learned how the court appeals process works. My case gave me some hope that there is some foundation in our history that supports and protects the rights of minorities. After all, the Bill of Rights was made to protect the rights of minorities.

Would you do the same thing today?

Yes.

How did this experience affect your life?

It has placed me in a position to talk about the issue of free speech for thirty years. I have been especially happy to talk to young people. I've worked in my professional and personal life as an advocate for young people. I believe very strongly that the rights of children must extend to the rights of decent housing, safe, clean neighborhoods, adequate health care, and good education.

What If?

What if *Tinker vs. Des Moines* came up before the Supreme Court today?

In 1988 students from Missouri believed that their First Amendment rights had been violated when school officials refused to let them print two articles in the school newspaper. They appealed their case all the way to the Supreme Court.

The makeup of the Court had changed by then and only two of the justices who had voted in favor of the Des Moines students were still on the court. What did the Court decide? Read *Hazelwood School District vs. Kuhlmeier* and find out.

Author's Note

The material in this book was edited from legal documents—the trial transcript, briefs, oral arguments before the U.S. Supreme Court, and judicial opinions. For purposes of economy, much material was edited. But the most important facts have been included to give a balanced picture so that you could be a fair judge.

Though Dan Johnston represented the students in all proceedings, Melvin L. Wulf of the American Civil Liberties Union and David N. Ellenhorn worked with Johnston in preparing the brief to the Supreme Court. Roy Lucas and Charles Morgan, Jr., representing the U.S. National Students Association, filed an *amicus brief*—a brief in support of the students as a "friend of the court."

Newspaper articles traced the case from the suspensions to the trial in district court, including direct quotes by various citizens. To re-create the atmosphere of the trial, the plaintiffs and their lawyer shared how they felt then. Unfortunately, except for Richard Moberly, the defendants and their lawyers are no longer alive, and the newspaper accounts provided little on their feelings.

Acknowledgments

I thank Alan H. Levine, who took time from his busy teaching schedule—and from his commitment to providing legal protection to all Americans—to read this manuscript. I thank Dan Johnston for critiquing the manuscript and answering many follow-up questions. Jonah Berg, Mary Chestaro, Kenton Kirby, Suzanna Rahman, and Malik Sharif of the Center School in Manhattan were ruthlessly honest in critiquing this book. Lori Morgan, Deputy Clerk, U.S. District Court, Southern District of Iowa, dug out the trial transcript for me. The U.S. Supreme Court library provided access to the other legal materials. Chris Farley, executive director of the Iowa Civil Liberties Union, and Marie Wilson, executive director of the Ms. Foundation, helped me track down Dan Johnston. Bob Rosegarten and Mildred Hoffman lent political buttons. The Des Moines Independent Community School District generously allowed me to wander through its schools, sit in classes, and speak with teachers, staff, and students; it also shared visual material essential to the book. Special thanks to Barbara Prior, executive director of Middle and High Schools; Dr. Michael Loffredo, principal of Warren Harding Junior High School; Dr. Joan Roberts, principal, Ginny Renda, vice principal, and Marge Overholser, secretary, of North High School; and Dr. Jerry Conley, principal of Theodore Roosevelt High School. Melinda Voss of the *Des Moines Register* and co-chair of the Visiting Scholars Program of the Roosevelt Parents-Faculty Club invited me to Des Moines to attend the Visiting Scholar sessions. Louise Rosenfield-Noun enriched my perception of the Des Moines community.

Mary Grefe and Dick Moberly graciously agreed to be interviewed for the book. The plaintiffs and their families offered cherished memorabilia—letters, articles, and photographs—to be used in this book. Marjorie Eckhardt and Lorena Jeanne Tinker shared important memories. My deepest thanks to Chris Eckhardt, Dan Johnston, John Tinker, and Mary Beth Tinker, who shared their memories and feelings, clarified bothersome details, and enriched my life as well as the material in this book. And as always, I am grateful to everyone at HarperCollins.

Bibliography

Books

The starred (*) books are particularly appropriate for young readers.

*Carey, Eve.; Levine, Alan H.; Price, Janet R. *The Rights of Students: The Basic ACLU Guide to Students' Rights.* Carbondale and Edwardsville, Illinois: Southern Illinois University Press, 1988.

*Epstein, Sam and Beryl. *Kids in Court.* New York: Four Winds Press, 1982.

*Hentoff, Nat. *The First Freedom.* New York: Delacorte Press, 1980.

Lewis, Anthony. *Gideon's Trumpet.* New York: Vantage Books, 1964.

Rosenfield-Noun, Louise. *Journey to Autonomy: A Memoir.* Ames, Iowa: Iowa State University Press, 1990.

Legal Documents

Brief for the Petitioners, October Term 1968, Dan L. Johnston, Melvin L. Wulf, David N. Ellenhorn, Attorneys for Petitioners

Brief for the Respondents, October Term 1968, Allan A. Herrick, Herschel G. Langdon, David W. Belin, Philip C. Lovrien, Attorneys for the Respondents

Judicial decisions: *Blackwell vs. Issaquena County Board of Education*, 363 F. 2nd 749 (1966); *Brown vs. Louisiana*, 383 U.S. 131 (1966); *Burnside vs. Byars*, 363 F. 2nd 744, (5th Circuit, 1966); *Tinker vs. Des Moines Independent Community School District*, 393 U.S. 503 (1966); Court Opinion, U.S. District Court for the Southern District of Iowa, Central Division, September 1, 1966, Roy L. Stephenson, Chief Judge; *West Virginia Board of Education vs. Barnette*, 319 U.S. 624 (1943).

Oral Arguments, U.S. Supreme Court, Washington, D.C., November 12, 1968

Trial Transcript, *Tinker vs. Des Moines Independent Community School District*, Des Moines, Iowa, July 25, 1966

Newspapers

Des Moines Register
Des Moines Sunday Register
Des Moines Tribune

Law Clerk's Notes

These notes cover only trial testimony, judicial decisions, appeals briefs, and all arguments, because that is all you, as a judge, are allowed to see.

Page numbers in *italics* refer to illustrations.

Doreen Rappaport

is the author of many books for children, including two other books in the *Be the Judge • Be the Jury* series: THE LIZZIE BORDEN TRIAL and THE SACCO-VANZETTI TRIAL; LIVING DANGEROUSLY: *American Women Who Risked Their Lives for Adventure*; ESCAPE FROM SLAVERY: *Five Journeys to Freedom*, a 1991 Notable Children's Trade Book in the Field of Social Studies (NCSS/CBC); THE BOSTON COFFEE PARTY; TROUBLE AT THE MINES, an Honor Book for the 1988 Jane Addams Children's Book Award; and AMERICAN WOMEN: *Their Lives in Their Words*, a 1990 Notable Children's Trade Book in the Field of Social Studies (NCSS/CBC) and a 1992 ALA Best Book for Young Adults.

Ms. Rappaport lives in New York City. When she is not writing, she is dreaming about traveling or hip-hop dancing.